50 Things Not to Do after 50

50 Things Not to Do after 50

From Naming Your Pets after Tolkien Characters to Signaling
"Peace Out" to Your Friends

Leland Gregory

Skyhorse Publishing

Skyhorse Publishing books may be purchased in bulk at special discounts for sales promotion, corporate gifts, fund-raising, or educational purposes. Special editions can also be created to specifications. For details, contact the Special Sales Department, Skyhorse Publishing, 307 West 36th Street, 11th Floor, New York, NY 10018 or info@skyhorsepublishing.com.

Skyhorse® and Skyhorse Publishing® are registered trademarks of Skyhorse Publishing, Inc.®, a Delaware corporation.

Visit our website at www.skyhorsepublishing.com.

10 9 8 7 6 5 4 3 2 1

Library of Congress Cataloging-in-Publication Data is available on file.

Cover design by Jane Sheppard
Cover photo credit Thinkstock
Illustrations by Dennis Cox/Thinkstock

Print ISBN: 978-1-62914-430-6
Ebook ISBN: 978-1-62914-847-2

Printed in China

This book is dedicated to my mother, Jenny, and my father, "The Colonel." Thank you for tolerating me during my teenage years and beyond and for not smothering me with a pillow while I slept. Also, thanks for having me or else I never would have grown up, become 50, and been able to write this book.

Acknowledgments

I would like to thank my editor, Holly Rubino, as well for not smothering me with a pillow while I slept. I also want to thank the following people for supplying me with some material for this book: Mike Long, Mary Louise McKinney, Julia Rose Coale, Randy Cassingham, and Edward Feuerherd. I'm not saying who is 50 years old or not, but you know who you are ☺.

Introduction

If you're turning 50, or have recently turned 50, or you've been 50 for a while and have just been lying about your age, then this book is both for you and about you. First, congratulations on this major accomplishment. From the 1500s to around the year 1800, life expectancy throughout the world hovered between the ages of 30 and 40 (and, in some countries, even less). Having turned 50 myself, I thought I would put together a list of things you should or shouldn't do when you reach this ripe, old age (even though I've always thought it was insulting to use the word "ripe" when talking about old people). Don't get me wrong. I'm not telling you not to do certain things. I'm only making suggestions, so don't get your Depends in a wad.

Turning 50 is not so bad considering the alternative. Hopefully we are wiser, have overcome our destructive behaviors (at least some of them), have learned from our mistakes (or learned to make different ones), have realized some of our dreams, and have not given up on the others. This is an age to rejoice. We are the survivors. So take this book in the playful manner in which it was written and with a grain of salt—but not more than a grain because you need to watch your blood pressure. I had so much fun taking potshots at people in their fifties that I've included ten more bits of advice as a bonus. The truth is, I lost count. Anyway, since I enjoy dispensing unsolicited advice, you get 60 for the price of 50. Lucky you.

I thought I'd leave you with some fun facts about turning 50:

- If you are exactly 50, then you have been on this earth for 18,262 days, or 438,288 hours, or 26,297,280 minutes, or 1,577,836,800 seconds. Doesn't that make you feel a little younger, especially when you start running the same numbers on the Earth, which is estimated to be 4.54 billion years old?
- Using an average heart rate of 72 beats per minute, your heart has beaten around 1,893,404,160 times during your lifetime so far. Doing something nearly 2 billion times has got to be exhausting. So go ahead. Take that nap.
- Taking the average of twelve breaths per minute, at a rate about one-fourth of a cubic foot of air, means you breathe approximately 388 cubic feet of air in a day. So during your 50 years so far you've inhaled and exhaled approximately 7,085,656 cubic feet of air. When someone accuses you of being full of hot air . . . well, you are.

50 Things Not to Do after 50

Even if it's become an accepted topic at cocktail parties, refrain from talking about your colonoscopy or asking people about theirs. It doesn't make for pleasant dinner conversation and it conjures up nightmarish images for people who haven't had one yet. When you were younger, poo poo jokes were funny, but you're beyond that now. Besides, colonoscopies are nothing to laugh at (fart jokes, however, will always have a timeless appeal).

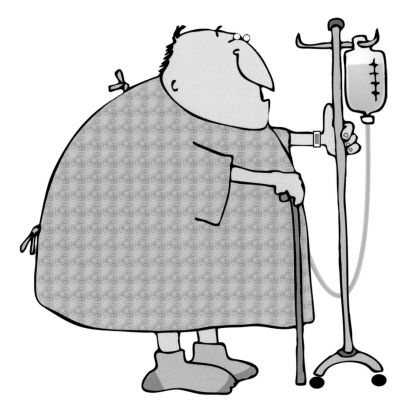

Avoid making a Facebook account for your dog. If you're a woman and have more than three cats, don't identify them as "children" on your Facebook page. Facebook is, however, a great way to find people you haven't seen in a while. Remember, though, that the boy or girl you had a major crush on in high school does not look the way you might remember him or her. He or she, too, has been smashed by the hammer of time.

If you're running around the house naked (which I condone), and someone calls, please, please, don't tell them you're running around the house naked. From an outsider's point of view, you probably resemble Jell-O in a paint shaker. There. I said it. I'm sorry.

"Nobody expects to trust his body overmuch after the age of fifty." —Alexander Hamilton, founding father and dude on the $10 bill

Shooting fake gang signs is not for 50-year-olds. Your twelve-year-old niece will only play along for so long before she tells all her friends what a dork you are. Also, if you don't know sign language, there's no telling what you're actually saying.

Now is not the time to do things you've never trained to do, like climb Mount Kilimanjaro, swim the English Channel, or enter a weight lifting competition. Face it, your mind and body are completely separate entities. The mind will try to convince you that you still have the abilities you had in your twenties, but your body is the realist. Take this simple test: pick up a cushion from the couch and run from one end of your house to the other as quickly as you can. If you're out of breath, put the cushion back on the couch, sit down, and turn on the television. If you're not huffing and puffing, then you might consider the previously mentioned activities.

Don't let this happen to you:

Mountaineer Reinhold Messner of Bolzano, Italy, who was the first man to scale Mount Everest without oxygen, broke a bone in his heel at his home. It was rumored that the 50-year-old man was injured when he scaled the wall after locking himself out.

You may have been practicing yoga since your twenties (bully for you!), but this does not give you the right to gesture "namaste" at complete strangers. This prayer and bow combo will only make you come off as highly insincere, and no one cares about the divine spark in your heart chakra anyway.

Don't complain about the lyrics in modern music. Remember, you used to listen to "Surfin' Bird" by the Trashmen, "Louie Louie," and "MacArthur Park." There's always been good music, and there's always been bad. I'm sure your parents thought the music of their generation was the best. Here's some advice: if you don't like modern music, don't listen to it. On the flip side, it is weird to see a 50-year-old man in a Buick blasting gangsta rap on his way to the golf course.

Stop calling yourself middle age unless half the people you know are over 100.

Don't let this happen to you:

Fifty-year-old bricklayer Alex Mitchell died laughing while watching the "Kung Fu Kapers" episode from the British comedy television series, *The Goodies*. After twenty-five minutes of continuously laughing at a kilt-clad Scotsman battling a vicious black pudding with his bagpipes, Mitchell gave one last "tremendous belly laugh, slumped on the settee, and died," said his widow. Mrs. Mitchell, it was reported, later sent a fan letter to *The Goodies* thanking them for making Mitchell's final moments of life so pleasant.

Now is not the time to join the mile-high club. At your age, if you try to have sex on a plane, you'll just throw your back out. However, if you do have sex on a plane, it's a good thing there's always an oxygen mask nearby. Just remember to always return your partner to the full upright and locked position.

It's probably too late to attempt to learn Einstein's theory of relativity, so don't even try. Heck, you can't even remember where you left your keys, let alone do complex equations. It's actually a blessing that the mind is the first thing to go. It relieves us of the misery of watching our bodies fall apart. Forgetfulness has its advantages . . . I just can't remember what they are right now.

This is a bad time in your life to suddenly get hooked on video games. I'm not talking about playing a harmless game of "Angry Birds" or "Candy Crush" while you're in the back of a taxi, waiting on an appointment, or even at the funeral of someone you never really liked. I'm talking about staying up forty-eight hours in a row, eating peanut butter crackers, and peeing in an empty two-liter soda bottle while engrossed in a MMORPG.* The only level you need to get to is an acceptable cholesterol level.

---

*Massively multiplayer online role-playing game (didn't want you to have to look it up).

Even though you now have more hair on your back (and in your ears and nose) than you do on your head, don't get yourself into a dander about it. Another bit of advice is not to piss off your wife right before she waxes your back (don't ask how I know this). It is, however, different for women who are losing their hair. But ladies, please resist the urge to wear a platinum, purple, orange, yellow, or pink wig. It won't make you look younger; it will only look like you were involved in a paint fight and lost. Remember the term "blue hair"? Don't be that woman.

Don't worry if it takes longer to rest than it did to get tired. You probably need the rest. Don't let it bother you if friends and visitors notice that one side of the couch is lower to the ground, and that the cushion has a permanent impression of your butt.

"I don't believe that when you are 25 you are over the hill. Fifty is the new 30." —Michael Flatley, Irish American dancer

Don't drive like a teenager. Why? Because you're not a teenager. Even though you probably have better insurance, your reaction time is slower. And at your age, what could you possibly be in a hurry about? You should also resist the impulse to buy an ATV or a motorcycle. A Rascal or Hoveround is now more your speed.

Don't let this happen to you:

While trying to reach the controls of the access fence at his gated community, a 52-year-old in Tobyhanna, Pennsylvania, fell out of his truck and then accidentally ran over himself.

No one is interested in how much or how little sleep you got last night. Don't ask, don't tell.

Don't let this happen to you:

Jim Harris, 56, was relaxing in the recliner in his Tavernier, Florida, home when he leaned over to turn on the lamp—and kapow!—Bubba fell on him. Bubba was the 200-pound stuffed head of a water buffalo that was mounted on his wall. Harris was unconscious for two hours, and it took four rescuers to get Bubba off him. "I guess it's payback for the buffalo, but I'm not even the guy who shot him," Harris said. "So embarrassing to get my ass kicked by a dead water buffalo."

The time for twerking has passed. It wasn't a word when you were young enough to do it, and now that it has acquired a name, you shouldn't be seen doing it in public (actually, you shouldn't even try this at home). If you have to look up what it means, you definitely shouldn't be doing it. I don't want you to bruise yourself—or your ego.

"I'm aiming by the time I'm fifty to stop being an adolescent." —Charles Caleb Colton, English cleric

Now is not the time in your life when you should quit your job in order to "get the band back together."

Don't let this happen to you:

The *Milwaukee Sentinel* reported that funeral companies are getting requests for more classic rock than classical music at funeral services. Local funeral director Mark Krause said, "For one young man, we played Led Zeppelin all night long. I think some of the older people were uncomfortable, but the boy's friends totally embraced it." Krause added, "We even had a biker funeral where they played 'Born to Be Wild.'"

Do not give in to the velour tracksuit! If someone buys one for you as a gift, do not wear it, especially if you have large thighs because, with the friction, you will be considered a fire hazard. One more thing: If there's enough room on the seat of the pants for the word "Bootylicious," you have to be honest with yourself that you're just not.

Don't volunteer to be a drug mule.

Don't let this happen to you:

Patricia Edwards, 51, was identified as the woman who entered a Bank of America in Sanford, Florida, handed the teller a hold-up note, then walked out without any money. After being arrested, Edwards confessed, "There was no plan, no nothing, just impulse. I think everyone should have a list of things they want to do before they die."

At 50, you have probably and unfortunately lost some old friends. The good news is that by the time you turn 50, you have gained a few new friends. However, your doctor, cardiologist, dentist, nurse, and all the people on the hospital staff don't count.

The socks-with-sandals look is a definite fashion "don't" after 50. German tourists have been trying to perfect this look for decades with no success. In fact, unless you're at the beach, you should never wear sandals at all, especially if you're a man. Have you looked at your toenails lately? The seagulls might mistake them for corn chips.

Women, I want to spare you from having to find out for yourselves that "Victoria's secret" means no one your age looks good in a thong. And men, Speedos (aka "banana hammocks") not only make you look desperate, they're just gross, plain and simple.

One good thing about turning 50 is that most of the embarrassingly stupid stuff you did was pre-Internet. So now is not the time to start posting incriminating Polaroids on Throwback Thursday.

Despite the norms of social etiquette, I am happy to tell you that after 50, you no longer have to hold in your farts. However, proceed with caution because at your age sometimes a fart is much more than just a fart.

"By the time we hit fifty, we have learned our hardest lessons. We have found out that only a few things are really important. We have learned to take life seriously, but never ourselves."
—Marie Dressler, actress

You're still hot, but only in flashes. The only advantage to hot flashes is that they can make you pretend you're on a very short vacation in the tropics. If you're on a first date, don't tell the man you're with that you're having a hot flash. Men really don't understand what these are. Just fan yourself and say his charming ways are heating you up.

Although you might make enough money now it's not a good idea to start using crack or anything else that requires a pipe. Pipes haven't been cool since your grandfather's time—and crack is expensive these days.

Men, please don't think you're sexy enough to hit on 20-something girls. And women, please don't try to compete with the 20-something girls.

"One has to be able to count if only so that at fifty one doesn't marry a girl of twenty." —Maxim Gorky, writer

Don't be caught wearing mini-skirts or short shorts, as there are many things about you that are no longer mini.

"Looking fifty is great—if you're sixty." —Joan Rivers

Don't become that person who doesn't care what she wears when she goes to the store.

Although there is the promise of free candy, there is also the potential of being arrested if you decide to go trick-or-treating by yourself. Heed my advice and don't. If you really have the urge to dress up as a superhero, save it for the next Comic-Con. However, if you're lucky enough to find someone else who likes to play dress-up then throw caution to the wind. But for everyone's sake, stay in your own house.

Even though it can be fun, exciting, and a little naughty, don't play hide-and-seek with your spouse or your date. At your age you might forget to look for them.

Don't let this happen to you:

Welfare workers found a 50-year-old man living alone in a cave in the Ifsahan province in Iran. The man told the workers that he had moved there thirty years ago when his wife dumped him.

If you're divorced and have reentered the dating scene, do not bring up your ex-spouse during your date. Yes, we know your former husband or wife was the worst person in the world, but talking about him or her immediately conjures images of you doing the horizontal tango with someone else. Not a very appealing thing to think about, especially before the appetizers arrive.

If you're single in your fifties, your dwelling place should reflect your maturity. Now is not the time to try to relive your college days. There's nothing wrong with a vinyl record collection but just don't have them stored and displayed in plastic milk crates. And give up the harem motif. Scarves draped over lamp-shades and beaded curtains may have been sexy in your twenties but now they just make you look like you're a crazy tarot card reader.

Don't worry about the fact that you feel terrible in the morning and you didn't even stay out the night before. Gone are the days when you could party until 4am and then be at work bright and early at 8. No more carousing the bars at night and doing the walk of shame the next morning. In fact, "getting any" now refers to sleep.

"The real sadness of fifty is not that you change so much but that you change so little." —Max Lerner, American journalist

Don't go to Oktoberfest, especially if you have an overactive bladder. Although it might seem like a good idea at the time, don't volunteer to dress as a Barmädchen (German for "bar maid") and deliver heavy steins of beer to everyone. The women at the Hofbräuhaus in Munich have forearms like lumberjacks.

Don't let this happen to you:

Fifty-five-year-old Donald Wolfe of Brookville, Pennsylvania, was charged with public drunkenness after neighbors reported seeing him give mouth-to-mouth resuscitation to a roadkill possum along Route 36.

Make a list of all the old-sounding expressions your parents used to say—you know, the ones that made you roll your eyes. Keep the list in your pocket and whenever you actually say one of those things to your children or grandchildren, put $10 in a jar. At the end of the year, take a trip to Paris.

There's no need to spend money on braces. You've had crooked teeth all your life, and the teeth you still have won't be there much longer.

"At fifty, everyone has the face he deserves." —George Orwell, novelist

Don't throw a kegger. You might feel limber enough to do the limbo after you've consumed mass quantities of beer, and you might be successful at physically answering the question, "How low can you go?" But the next morning you'll be dealing with the other meaning of limbo—that is, hovering around the edges of hell.

It's not a good idea to share what negative effects certain types of food have on your digestive system. If green beans give you gas, don't eat them. If asparagus makes your pee stink, who cares? It makes everyone's pee stink. This is good advice, especially if you have recently reentered the dating scene. The things you used to freely tell your spouse are not things you should tell a new acquaintance, especially if you're trying to get him or her into bed. Also, don't order any menu items that include the words "grande," "super," "monster," "enormous," or "supreme," or end with the suffix "-zilla."

Don't go hot-tubbing with young people! It will only embarrass you and make everyone else feel uncomfortable and slightly nauseous.

If you still have a ponytail at your age it's time to let it go, especially if you're bald on top. This is called a "skullet" (like a mullet but with no "business in the front"), and no matter how cool you think it looks, from the back, you resemble a horse's rear end.

"After a man is fifty, you can fool him by saying he is smart, but you can't fool him by saying he's pretty."
—E. W. House

Don't try to pretend you're starting a new fashion statement when the reality is you got dressed without your glasses.

"When I was young, I was told, 'You'll see, when you're fifty.' I am fifty and I haven't seen a thing." —Erik Satie, composer and pianist

Now is not the time to try parkour. If you don't know what that is, great. If you do, don't do it. You'll break something.

"Everyone has talent at twenty-five. The difficulty is to have it at fifty." —Edgar Degas, artist

Although it's tempting, resist the urge to start embezzling from your company or planning a major heist. I know you've seen a lot of movies in which it looks easy, but you're no character played by Matt Damon or Catherine Zeta-Jones.

At your age it's normal for your vision to need some help. So don't worry about it. Just hold your head up high (hint: holding your head up high makes it easier to see through your trifocals).

"God grant me the senility to forget the people I never liked, the good fortune to run into the ones I do, and the eyesight to tell the difference." —Anonymous

F
M B
W V H J L
mnbvczx
Z V U C G K L A
jasdfgteknmnbvcamzx
asdfhkjjjhynigettttbctsdewwqa
mnbvcxqwertyuiopmahjstyetrtyyuiponcdsaaa

A duel at this age with any kind of weapon is not a good way of resolving your dispute with the next-door neighbor who won't return your lawnmower.

Whatever you do, don't buy a talking scale. You certainly don't want people in the next room hearing your weight, and it wouldn't help your self-esteem to hear the scale groan, "Get off me, tubby!"

"Middle age is when your age starts to show around your middle." —Anonymous

Now is not a good time to get drunk and give your boss a piece of your mind. You would make a pitiful pizza delivery person.

I recommend keeping your creative juices alive by taking an art class, but trust me, people don't want an unsolicited portrait of them that looks like a Picasso but wasn't supposed to.

Do your heart a favor and don't shovel your own driveway and sidewalk. That's what having kids was for. There are an estimated 1,200 reports of heart attacks attributed to snow shoveling. Even if your heart is in good shape, it's a good excuse to get out of doing that chore.

Just because your kids are grown and out of the house doesn't mean the children at the preschool or the old folks at the retirement home will appreciate a surprise visit from Santa Claus—especially if it's in July.

The main thing one should never do after the age of 50: COMPLAIN. You're still here, aren't you?!

"The years between fifty and seventy are the hardest. You are always being asked to do things, and yet you are not decrepit enough to turn them down." —T. S. Eliot

There's nothing wrong with reliving things from your childhood that gave you joy. A lot of people get back into model trains or start collecting Barbie dolls, but don't get carried away.

"I think when the full horror of being fifty hits you, you should stay home and have a good cry." —Josh Billings, humorist

Some people our age like to start a new hobby like collecting things. Some people collect stamps, coins, autographs, and porcelain figurines, but please, please, even though it seems like your body is falling apart, don't start collecting other people's body parts.

You're never too old to go back to college. You are, however, too old to date a college freshman, go to too many rush parties, or try out for the football team.

I'm projecting way off into the future here, but please don't request a bagpipe player at your funeral. It's not a pleasant sound, and it reminds people in their fifties about Spock's death, which is great if they're Trekkies, but for everyone else, not so much.

Remember, you may be an accountant, a supervisor, a lawyer, or even a candlestick maker, but a farmer you're not. Even though it might sound romantic to suddenly become one in your fifties, it's a bad idea. Just think of the flies!

Home improvement projects are a great way to keep your mind and your body active, but just be careful you don't do more harm than good.

Don't let this happen to you:

A man working on a roof at a high-rise slipped and was inevitably going to fall to his death when the pneumatic nail gun he was holding accidentally went off and nailed his pant leg to the roof. Rescue workers told the man to keep his pants on, and they were able to quickly pull him back to safety.

Now that you're in your fifties, you're secure with who you are (hopefully). But that doesn't mean you should express this with body piercings or a tattoo. Now, before you blow a gasket, I don't have anything against tattoos. But sacral tattoos (you know, the ones above your butt crack), tribal tattoos, or tattoo sleeves can be explained as follies of youth (remember, it's *girl* with the dragon tattoo) or, more usually, excessive alcohol consumption. If you do decide to have a tattoo, please don't get one on your head, face, or neck. You might think it's symbolic but everyone else will think you've finally snapped.

Now is the time to stop saying, "That makes me feel old." You are officially old. Prepare to hear these terrifying words from your doctor: "You're in pretty good shape for a person your age."

50 Things Not to Say after 50

One thing that will make you look and sound older in the minds of younger people is using the vernacular of the current generation. Words that haven't been cool or groovy for decades will also make you easily identifiable as old. In an effort to protect you from embarrassment, I have put together this list of things not to say after 50.

1. Neat
2. All that and a bag of chips
3. Swag
4. Dude
5. Par-tay
6. To the max
7. Not!
8. Totes
9. Freakin'
10. Hottie
11. Catch you on the flip-side
12. LOL
13. I'm like
14. That's *sick!*
15. Whatever
16. Kick it
17. Chill out
18. As if
19. I heart you
20. Hella (anything)
21. Can you dig it?
22. Fo'shizzle
23. Besties
24. BFF
25. Cray-cray

26. Doe
27. Groovy
28. Boss
29. BMOC
30. The Man
31. What's the dillio?
32. Cha-CHING!
33. Fly
34. I'm going to the little girls' room
35. Cool beans
36. Dat
37. Am I right, ladies?
38. Far out
39. Homey/homeslice
40. Knarly
41. Da bomb
42. Talk to the hand
43. OMG
44. Open up a can of whoop-ass
45. Killin' it
46. You go, girl!
47. I can't even
48. Dag
49. Bogue
50. It's all good

50 Things Not to Wear after 50

As your body changes, so should your clothes. Ladies, please don't raid your daughter's closet looking for something hip to wear. You don't have the right hips for it anymore. And men, please don't think you'll look edgy by wearing the newest fashions. The only thing you'll look is out of place. Here are two lists of fashion don'ts for women and men after 50.

Women:

1. Crocs
2. Miniskirts
3. Purses with dogs on them or in them
4. Low-rise pants
5. Skinny jeans
6. Jeggings (aka "jean leggings")
7. T-shirts that say "Sexy grandma"
8. Gold name chains
9. Uggs
10. Jumpsuits
11. Fishnet stockings
12. Décolletage-revealing tops
13. Bright colored eye shadow
14. Shoes you can fall off of
15. Stirrup pants
16. Shoes with Velcro straps

17. Off-the-shoulder sweatshirts (à la *Flashdance*)
18. Tweed skirt suits
19. Brogues
20. Dirndls
21. Peasant blouses, peasant skirts
22. Gladiator sandals
23. Lurex dresses
24. Slacks
25. Any combination of beige/lilac/mint green

Men:

1. Crocs
2. Visors
3. Ed Hardy shirts
4. Bright sneakers
5. Winter shorts
6. Saggy jeans that reveal your boxers
7. Jean shorts (aka "jorts")
8. Speedos
9. Wallet chains
10. Leather wristbands
11. T-shirts with funny slogans or free ones from your local bank
12. Pooka shell necklaces
13. Capris
14. Overalls
15. Mock turtlenecks
16. Pointy-toed shoes
17. Skull jewelry
18. Fake tans
19. Flat-brimmed caps
20. Black sneakers
21. Short-sleeve button downs
22. Pleated pants
23. Novelty underwear
24. Wife beaters
25. Neon anything

You Can't Deny You're 50 When...

1. Your face has more wrinkles than an elephant's butt.
2. You're grateful when someone tells you there is lipstick on your teeth, as that means you still have your teeth (or at least they're still in).
3. You continue to keep four sizes of clothes in your closet, even though you know you'll never fit into three of them again.
4. You purchase your moisturizer by the case instead of by the jar.
5. The only way to take all the wrinkles out of your face is by taking off your bra.
6. A hot time now means either putting a heating pad on your back or Ben-Gay on your shoulders, or menopause.
7. The taxi driver says "Yes, ma'am" instead of "You got it, darlin'."

8. You often repeat things . . .
9. Looking into a full-length mirror, you can see your butt from the front.
10. The candles on your birthday cake cost more than the cake did.
11. You stop calling your wrinkles "laugh lines." Nothing is that funny.
12. The best way to keep up with your friends is by reading the obituaries.
13. Your address book is filled mostly with names that start with Dr.
14. Your concept of getting lucky changes from "having sex" to "not having to wake up at night to go pee."

15. The only reason you take Viagra is so you won't roll out of bed. Or you take half a Viagra so you don't pee on your shoes.
16. You now use the phrase "good grass" to refer to your neighbor's lawn.
17. You listen to Led Zeppelin's "Stairway to Heaven" and realize you're halfway up the stairway already.
18. You come to the realization that everything on your body that doesn't hurt doesn't work!
19. Your bad knee goes out more than you do.
20. You often repeat things . . .
21. Your chiropractor sends you birthday cards.

22. You would rather buy your own drinks than have to talk to that creepy guy for five minutes.
23. The only time you hear music from your generation is when you're in the elevator.
24. Functionality becomes a factor when purchasing undergarments.
25. You know where virtually every bathroom in the city is located.
26. The only exercise you get is serving as a pallbearer for your friends.
27. You realize with some reluctance that your father was right about nearly everything.
28. You make the transition from the Grateful Dead to grateful you're not dead.

29. You realize you've finally got it all together, but can't remember where you put it.
30. You and your teeth don't sleep together anymore.
31. While attempting to smooth out the wrinkles in your socks you realize you aren't wearing any.
32. While sitting down at the breakfast table you hear snap, crackle, pop and you're not eating cereal.
33. You realize that you finally do look like your passport photograph.
34. You often repeat things . . .
35. You look for your glasses for half an hour and they were on your head the whole time.

36. You see a cute member of the opposite sex and start calculating if you could be his or her mother or father.
37. You look at your watch three times in a row and still can't remember what time it is.
38. You buy a book to help you with your memory issues and then forget where you put it.
39. You have to prepare yourself mentally to get off the couch.
40. Your spouse whispers in your ear that he or she wants to go upstairs and make love, but you only have enough energy for one of those tasks.
41. People start referring to you as a grown-up because you groan every time you get up.
42. You often repeat things . . .

43. You seriously start considering buying a second medicine cabinet.
44. People put a mirror under your nose when you fall asleep on the couch.
45. Most of your sentences begin with, "When I was your age . . ."
46. You realize you're the only person in the room who knows what "rewind" means.
47. You look at pictures of your twenty-one-year old self, and your first thought is, "I was so skinny." Your second is remembering how fat you thought you were.
48. You look at the nutrition label on a Snicker's bar, calculate how many minutes you'd have to spend on the treadmill to burn it off, and decide it's just not worth it.
49. You no longer know every song on the radio or every artist in the Top 40.
50. You've had to look up Internet slang. KWIM?

Leland Gregory is the two-time *New York Times* bestselling author of *Stupid American History* and *America's Dumbest Criminals* and is a former writer for *Saturday Night Live.* Leland has authored more than thirty books, many of them national best sellers, including *Stupid History, The Stupid Crook Book,* and *What's the Number for 911?* He has written and sold a screenplay to Disney and optioned another screenplay to Touchstone. He was a co-creator of the nationally syndicated TV series "America's Dumbest Criminals." Leland is currently executive producer for the PBS series "Parsons Table" and served as executive producer for the PBS show "The Whole Truth."

He's created advertising campaigns for national corporations like Captain D's, International Paper, Dollar General, Cracker Barrel, and AT&T and has contributed to such publications as *Reader's Digest*, *George*, and *Maxim*.

He became a nationally recognized political media consultant in 1994 when his work helped a long-shot candidate beat an eighteen-year incumbent. In 2002 he was awarded the prestigious Gold Pollie award for Overall Television Campaigns for his work on a highly publicized Senate race.

Leland is an overall nice guy who has no interesting hobbies.